I

Dogs

Golden Retrievers

by Lisa Trumbauer

Consulting Editor: Gail Saunders-Smith, PhD

Consultant: Jennifer Zablotny, DVM
Member, American Veterinary Medical Association

Capstone press

Mankato, Minnesota

Pebble Books are published by Capstone Press,
151 Good Counsel Drive, P.O. Box 669, Mankato, Minnesota 56002.
www.capstonepress.com

1 2 3 4 5 6 11 10 09 08 07 06

Library of Congress Cataloging-in-Publication Data
Trumbauer, Lisa, 1963–
    Golden retrievers / by Lisa Trumbauer.
    p. cm.—(Pebble Books. Dogs)
    Summary: "Simple text and photographs present an introduction to the golden
retriever breed, its growth from puppy to adult, and pet care information"—
Provided by publisher.
    Includes bibliographical references and index.
    ISBN-13: 978-0-7368-5334-7 (hardcover)
    ISBN-10: 0-7368-5334-0 (hardcover)
    1. Golden retriever—Juvenile literature. I. Title. II. Series.
SF429.G63T78 2006
636.752'7—dc22   2005021594

Note to Parents and Teachers

The Dogs set supports national science standards related to life
science. This book describes and illustrates golden retrievers.
The images support early readers in understanding the text. The
repetition of words and phrases helps early readers learn new
words. This book also introduces early readers to subject-specific
vocabulary words, which are defined in the Glossary section. Early
readers may need assistance to read some words and to use the
Table of Contents, Glossary, Read More, Internet Sites, and Index
sections of the book.

Table of Contents

The Retriever

Golden retrievers have golden brown fur. They retrieve things for their owners.

Golden retrievers
help their owners.
They retrieve birds
for hunters.

From Puppy to Adult

Golden retriever puppies are small.
They have long tails and floppy ears.

Golden retriever puppies like to play fetch. They quickly learn to retrieve.

Puppies grow up fast.
Adult golden retrievers
are taller than
a park bench seat.

Golden Retriever Care

Golden retrievers should be brushed often.

Owners should take
golden retrievers
on long walks every day.

18

Golden retrievers need
dog food and
fresh water every day.

Golden retrievers do not
like to be alone.
They need people
to love them
and play with them.

Glossary

brush—to take out the knots from hair or fur; golden retrievers have long fur that should be brushed often.

fetch—a game of throwing a ball or stick and having a dog bring it back to you

hunter—someone who hunts animals for food or sport; golden retrievers help people who hunt birds.

retrieve—to bring something back

Read More

Murray, Julie. *Golden Retrievers*. Edina, Minn.: Abdo, 2003.

Patent, Dorothy Hinshaw. *The Right Dog for the Job*. New York: Walker and Company, 2004.

Internet Sites

FactHound offers a safe, fun way to find Internet sites related to this book. All of the sites on FactHound have been researched by our staff.

Here's how:

1. Visit *www.facthound.com*
2. Type in this special code **0736853340** for age-appropriate sites. Or enter a search word related to this book for a more general search.
3. Click on the **Fetch It** button.

FactHound will fetch the best sites for you!

Index

Word Count: 104
Grade: 1
Early-Intervention Level: 14

Editorial Credits

Martha E. H. Rustad, editor; Juliette Peters, designer; Wanda Winch, photo researcher; Scott Thoms, photo editor

Photo Credits

Brand X Pictures/Andersen Ross, 20; Bruce Coleman Inc./Ian and Karen Stewart, 1; Elite Portrait Design/Lisa Fallenstein-Holthaus, 12, 18; Mark Raycroft, 4, 6, 14, 16; PhotoEdit Inc./Frank Siteman, 10; Ron Kimball Stock/Ron Kimball, cover, 8